"i don't want to seem like a wanna-be"
"we are all wanna-bes"

playlist
spotify "all those things in playlist"

…in red
conan gray – **maniac**
i dont know how but they found me – **choke**
krewella – **calm down**
all time low – **monsters** ft. demi lovato and blackbear
missio – **kdv** ft. shug

…in blue
sara kays – **chosen last**
twenty one pilot – **trapdoor**
jacob lee – **demons**
a fine frenzy – **almost lover**
taylor swift – **death by a thousand cuts**

…in green
ruelle – **carry you** ft. fleurie
selena gomez – **people you know**
oh wonder – **happy**
avril lavigne – **souvenir**
anna blue – **where do i go**

…in purple
skillet – **lions**
the score – **in my bones**
one ok rock – **we are**
syml – **break free**
halsey – **nightmare**

contents

...in red

anger

living in an aquarium
everyone sees me
but no one knows me

all those things...

i told you
i am lonely
and you left me alone

your loss
leaving something permanently
for something temporarily

all those things…

i did not know
that parents are not allowed
by law
to leave their children
alone at home

i just went with it

you used my words against me

- used-to-be friend

all those things…

you never asked twice
not even once

when i am gone
the story of mine just starts

- the talks about me

i am the gasoline
for people's fire of hate

stop telling me
i can talk to you

every time i call you
at 3 am
no one is picking up

all those things…

stop telling me
what to do

it is like
you are telling me
i am not enough

when i lost ~~us~~ you

i lost
family
home
best friend
soulmate
sanctuary

do not tell me
you are suffering
as hard as me

you said
you do not know how to be romantic

i watched all the movies 'n series you told me to
i know all the books you told me about

so many things to be inspired of

so tell me
how do you not know how to be romantic?

"you need to know
what **he**
told **her**
about **you**"

- fake lover, fake friend

telling me
that you are embarrassed
by how i behave
does not make me
behave better next time

i know
he could have died

but i died

because you left me lonely
to save him

- you have two children

all those things...

"should i take the next train to you?"
stop making false hope

not even the help cries
on my body
did you recognize

welcome to the journey
of going through hell
seems like only
stupid, careless and selfish ones
can survive

- life

how could you
calling me useless?

- not born to serve

now
all i want to do is
the things you love

- read the books
- watch the TV shows
- listen to the music
- do the hobbies

just to be the person
you would love to have
by your side

just to make you regret
losing me

- rage

how could you
telling me
i was talking

BULLSHIT

when i was trying
to explain my feelings?

- another trauma

i hope
i am the best
you will ever have had

how can you
expect me to behave
how you want

when you were not even there
to help me build up my behavior?

she told me
you told her
you have never liked **my body** anyway

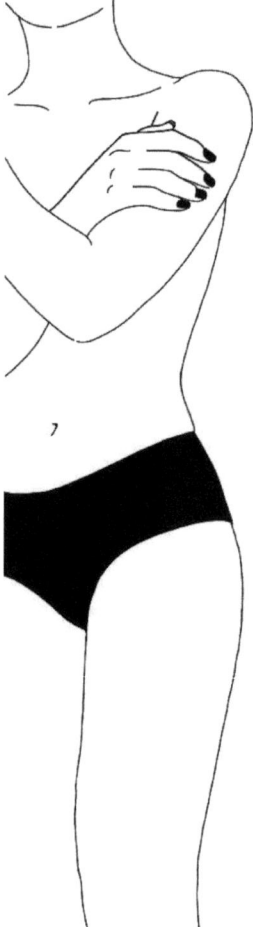

we were at the appointment with the doctor
my body was aching now and then

he prognosticated
i was not sick
but my mind was manipulating my body
to catch your attention
you did not give me
when your son was sick

you denied
"that is not possible
it is several years ago"

i hated it
when you said sorry
instead of improving

am i not worthy enough to try it better?

i know
you must have been tired
of taking care of my sick brother

but there is a trauma
of not being picked up

on the first day of kindergarten
on the first day of school
on the first day of violin lesson

because you forgot
~~your first born~~

could you even stand straight
when you feel the pain
you are causing me?

"my parents have never bought me
these kind of toys"
you said

"your parents did not need to keep you busy
alone at home"
i thought

dear cancer,
i wish you were only the favorite animal of
my brother

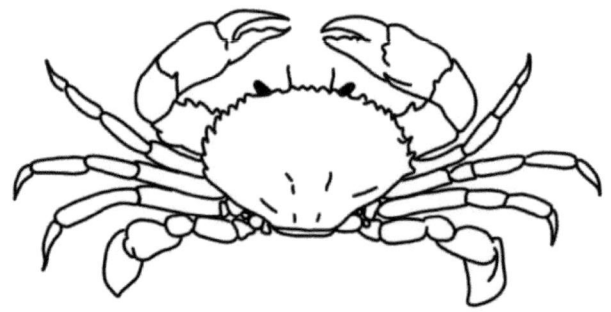

better cry every damn night
than have this all stuck inside

...in blue

sadness

will he love me less tomorrow?

in the middle of a storm
i found my shelter that keeps me away
from being hurt

why would i want to escape?
out there is a hurricane

in the middle of a storm
i found my shelter that keeps me safe

how can we be in the same room
but not with each other?
how can you say you love me without
meaning it?

you were not feeling it
but neither did i

i still love the person
you used to be

when will i meet her/him again?

heartache every time
he says
goodbye

all those things…

when the sun sets at 9 pm
it is time to be sad again

stuck in this house called broken home
stuck in the past which will not let me go

stuck in the fear of failing in the future
stuck in the words you throw at me like stones

and maybe that is all i want

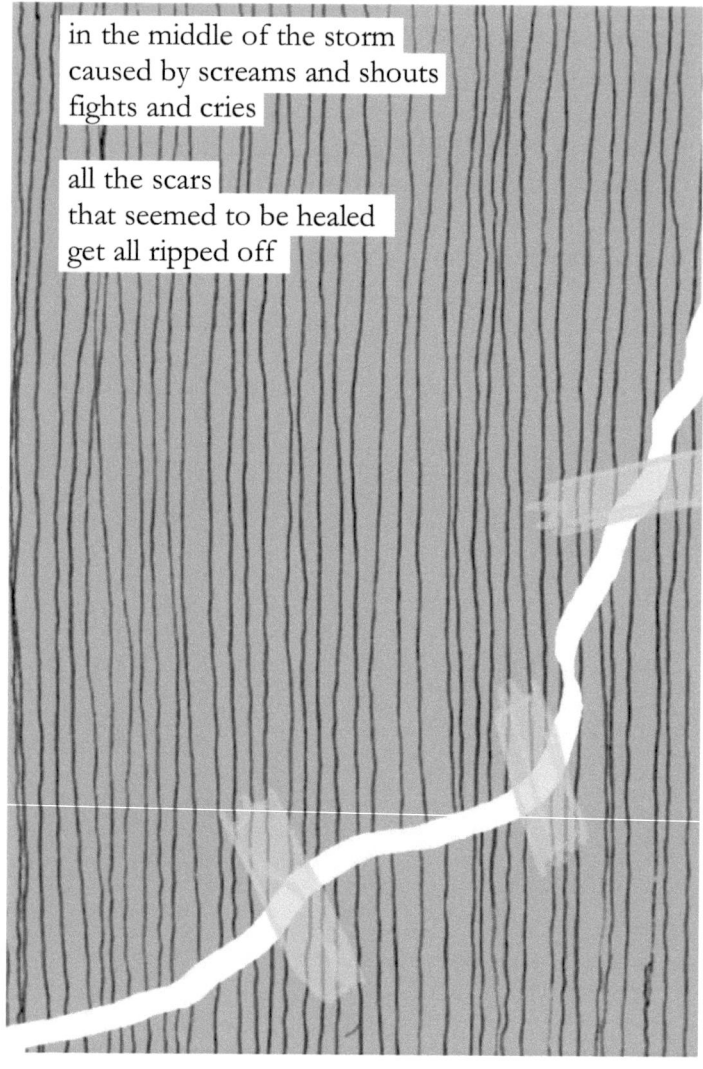

in the middle of the storm
caused by screams and shouts
fights and cries

all the scars
that seemed to be healed
get all ripped off

how can i heal in this broken home?

all those things…

you knew our expiration date

and i was claiming
we could be consumed forever

please tell me
are you going to
rescue me or
shoot me down?

all those things…

have i already consumed all my good karma?

do you check my

profile picture
status
the "online" sign?

because these are all for you

all those things…

it is like standing on a stage
but with a blind and deaf audience

talking is what they do

i do not like not feeling sad

and i cried

and cried

and cried

and cried

until i fell asleep

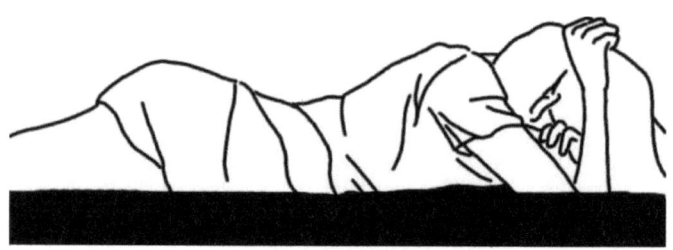

sitting in the dark
with chaos in my head
i cannot tame

all those things…

losing you is being homeless again

late at night
i cry
in Y O U R bed

all those things…

loneliness in togetherness

i want these thoughts to stay
they are making me feel special

- death wishes

a pleasant pain
made with scissors

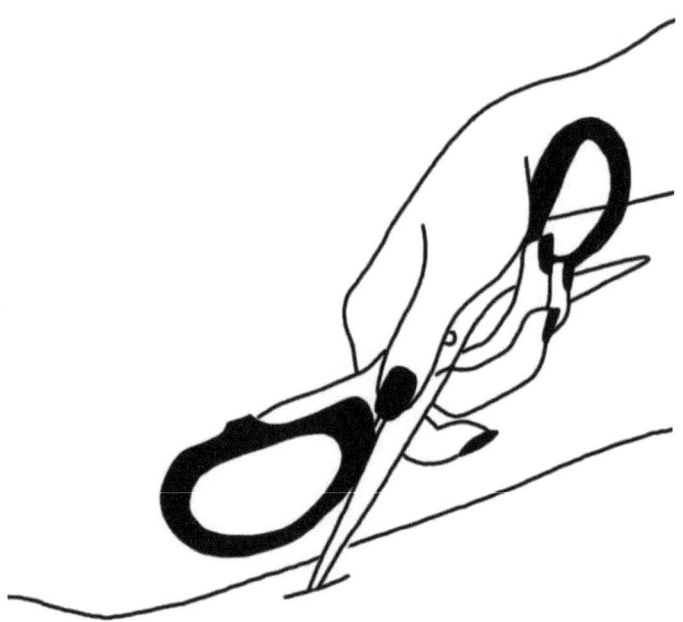

i hate my body
i hate my mind
i hate my soul
i hate my life

- a mantra

i want to be strong

strong enough to end this all

i just want to be distracted from my pain inside

please do not hang up the phone

all those things...

cry to sleep
is the best sleep

and apparently the only way

and then i screamed
but who the hell is able to read minds?

i wish i ended it all
the day i planned to

2017

i did not plan
to come this far

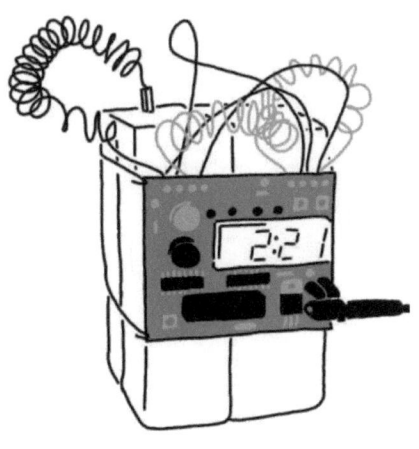

sleepless nights
tired eyes

mind full of chaos
heart full of pain

i am wasting this life

- a lullaby

are you already over us or
are you thinking about

how we used to be by each other's side?
how we used to love each other? and
how we used to make each other happy?

are you thinking about us or
am i the last standing warrior?

crossing the ocean of our tears
but still asking who cried the most

all those feelings on the inside
make me feel numb

a rescuer in my hand
making its mark

sometimes it bleeds
sometimes it does not

physical pain is better than mental pain

- we know, it is not a good solution

all those things…

"why haven't i died yet?"

- everyday thoughts

it feels like being set on fire

i wish to die in another way
because nothing hurts more than that

all those things…

it is barely possible to dance on this ground

i hate her
she does the same
- mirror

all those things…

where are you
when not in my head?

what are you thinking
when not about us?

"i love you" i said
"sorry" he responded

our last goodbye

- some breakups are not meant to be easy

i do not feel happiness
i cannot find happiness
there is no happiness

- self sabotage

all those things…

my mental fatigue is dragging down my
physique with it

i need to leave the place
i feel like dead

but the place is supposed
to be home

all those things...

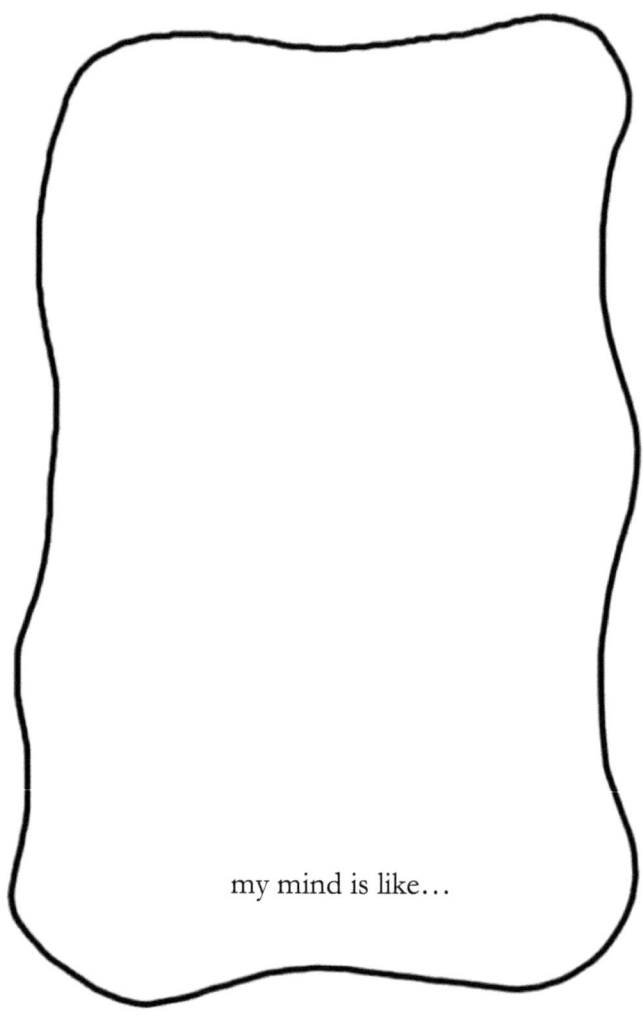

my mind is like...

...and sometimes like...

all those things…

"it is your home"
"it causes my scars"

at a certain point
i started to hate music

- this has gone way to far

all those things…

thinking about it is exhausting

i hate to sleep at night because sleeping means ending the day, means starting a new one and the new day could be a disaster. i just survived a day with this potential and it went fine. i do not want this to change.

all those things…

i lie in my bed
imagine you next to me
and i smile

and then i cry
you only exist in my memories

i wish you could see my pain
but you have never seen me in it

i cannot blame you

i want to be right every time i talk, i do, i write

like in an exam
you must study the solution first

- my type of an ideal way to live

i hate to be me
i hate to be like this

all those things…

don't wanna hurt
but don't wanna lie either

even when life is good for a moment
sometimes i am still fed up with it

all those things…

is it dead and gone forever
or is it somewhere waiting for us to return?

- our love

"maybe everyone who dies young knew it"
what a beautifully sad, but relieving theory

all those things...

you were the water
i was the flower

your ever-growing filth caused the death of me

i did not experience
rape
loss
accident
illness
abortion

but i still have the right to feel
sad
depressed
empty
angry
lost

- the personal doomsday

...in green

growth

i know i could have done so much
so many meaningful acts
so many successful achievements

but *things* are holding me back

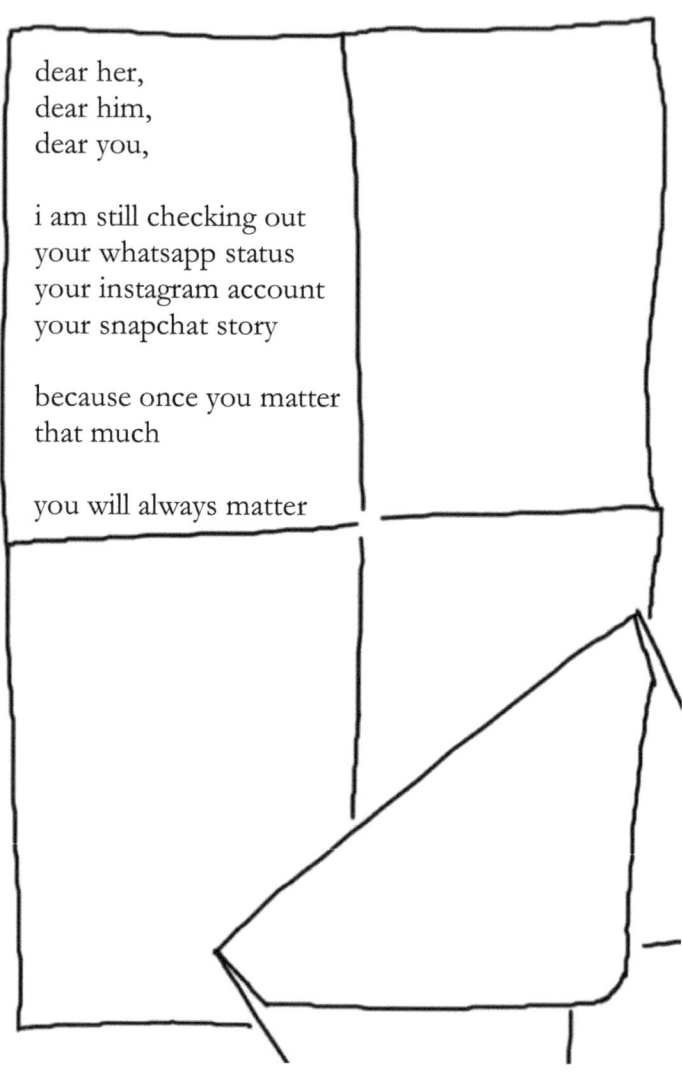

dear her,
dear him,
dear you,

i am still checking out
your whatsapp status
your instagram account
your snapchat story

because once you matter
that much

you will always matter

i wish
i could be
what i am
by heart

- cannot remember the script

i want to keep the number of people
who may not like me
as low as possible

i thought i am over you

but i saw you
being fully yourself
and i was still fascinated

- the proof i could have loved you until today

sorry i broke you first
but you broke me longer

i am hoping
for another universe
where we have our happily ever after

dear you,

i am trying to impress you
i am trying to make you jealous
it is toxic

goodbye

the moment
i realized
i loved you more
than myself
i needed to step up for myself again

i hate to see myself like this
i hate that no one sees me like this

- not weird at all

i wish you knew
i wish i told
i wish you asked

i want so many things
but at the same time
i want to lose everything

- correct or restart?

i regret
my first time
my first kiss
my first love

because these were with you

- hate might help to get over you

i was there
waiting for you
to make sure
you are not looking for me

- better safe than sorry

i want to see us smile again

i literally asked for a second chance
and you refused it

- why we are not likely to get back together

happiness should not be dependent

all those things…

i miss asking you how you are doing
i miss asking you what you are doing
i miss asking how your day was
i miss seeing you sent me a message

or maybe i just miss ~~you~~ the idea of being
in a relationship

i could not hold on to it longer
while you were still thinking
if it is what you wanted

even the water in the vase
needs to be kept clean
so the flower can grow healthy

- love

irono.yami

we could have avoided a number of
stupid things
but we also realized it when there was
no turning back

all those things…

what we had
was the definition of
toxic relationship/friendship

i did not know
why i was still holding on
to our friendship

even though
we became toxic
i could not let go

i did not know
that i was still hoping
for a better end

until you suddenly
cut off
our connection

hope dies last
but it dies

waiting and hoping
for the night
i can go sleep again
without crying

you never told me
what i am doing wrong

i never had the chance
to improve myself

kind of glad
it did not work out

all those things…

i know
i will be fine
but right now
imagine someone else
by my side
disgusts me

you slowly disgust me

all those things…

i have not seen the rainbow for a long time
i should turn around more often

.

i have never been to anywhere
i travelled a lot but
never enjoyed the moments

i have never been to anywhere
prisoned in my emptiness
time to break out

all those things...

i wish i mourned about you longer
but i need to move on

- finally

if one day
i want to remember us
i will know
where to find it
but hopefully
i will not have the urge

- usb stick

the moment
i saw my mother
crying over my scar art
on my body

i realized
that i am actually
hurting people
who see me suffer

i hope you realize that sooner

i loved being in a relationship
finding time for each other
making sacrifices
giving the best to impress

i should do these things for myself first

all those things…

we knew it secretly
all these time
we chose to ignore
the warning signs

i cannot remember
our nights
our kisses
our story

it makes me sad
not to know anymore

but i am certain
i would cry a river
if i still did

slowly but surely
i am finishing this puzzle

i thought i knew
the picture
by just seeing some pieces
but i am
putting these answers
together now

slowly but surely
it all makes
sense

the moment
i am dead to them
i start to live

all those things…

i am slowly overcoming
my personal doomsday

irono.yami

i write
to explain my world

you read
to find the explanation for yours

all those things…

slowly but surely
i stop thinking about
the "today a year ago with you"

i hope you do better
the next time
you find someone

i know our story is over
i just need time to heal

i have lost our memories
on my way to freedom

~~goodbye~~ farewell

there should be lip balm
for shattered hearts

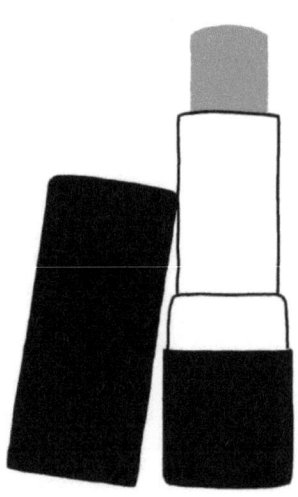

i used to struggle with
all those things
i wanted to do and to be

today i struggle with
the order of the things
i want to achieve next

why did i restrict myself?

i was surprised

when he said
"every day more"

to the question
"do you love me more than at the beginning
or now?"

because you said
"different"

- the proof you just had a crush

i wish
i could travel back
in time

and
help myself
to be back on my
feet again

rewriting memories
so exhausting
but necessary

i cannot wait to meet my soulmate
because it was not you

all those things…

recently i am happy
and i like it

i saw your eyes shining
when you were dancing and singing

tell me
does someone see that in mine too?

all those things…

oh love
how can you read me
like the headline?

i am your...
and
you are my...

...breaking news

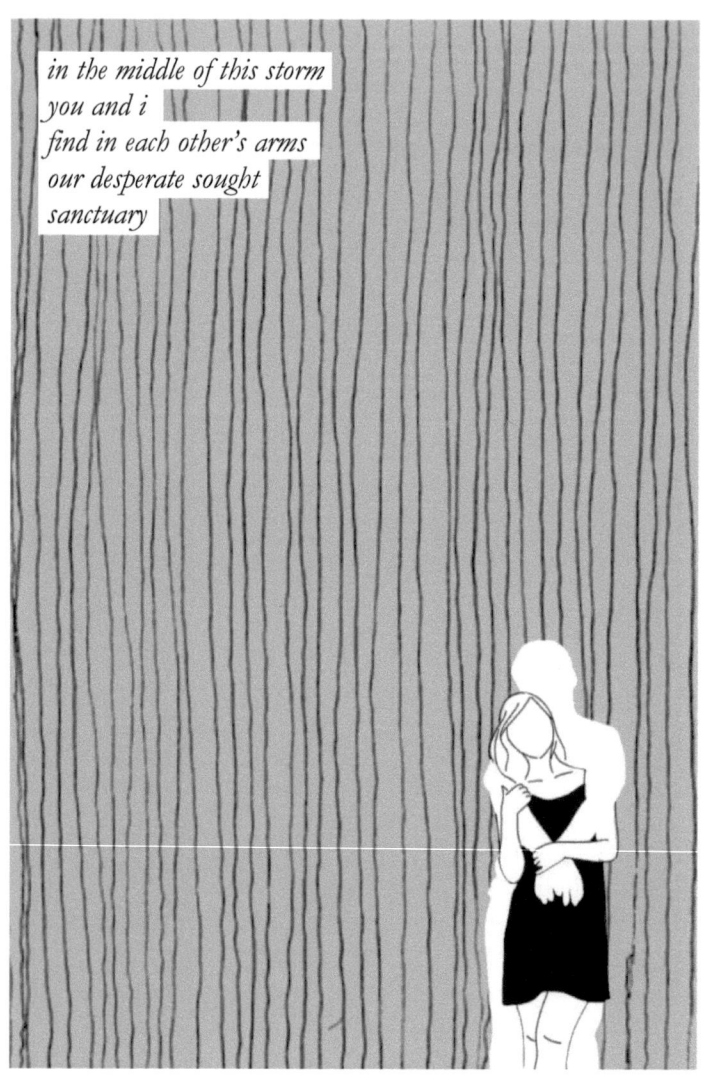

in the middle of this storm
you and i
find in each other's arms
our desperate sought
sanctuary

in the middle of this storm
you and i
find in each other's eyes
the sun again

all those things...

i will love you
~~*forever*~~
as long as i can

- forever is just a myth

thank you
for making me
being scared of dying

because it would mean
not to see and feel you
ever again

...in purple

wisdom

you do not have to experience cinematic tragedy to have the right of feeling sadness

beautiful and sad
mental illness is turning into art

beautiful and sad
they are still not taken seriously

a living being is not a collectible

all those things…

they gave you no reason to stay
they gave you no reason to leave

they gave you no reason to stay
this is reason enough to go

i do not know you
but yet
you can still relate
to my words

at the end
we, humans
are all the same
just in another phase of life

i see the smile of yours
but where do you hide
your sparkles and shines?

i see what you don't see
your arms wrapped around your demons

never let someone wait
just because you know
they will

one day
they won't

- game over

letting go hurts
but holding tight hurts even more

all those things...

did you know
friendship can be one-sided too?

finding time and *making* time is not the same

let that sink in

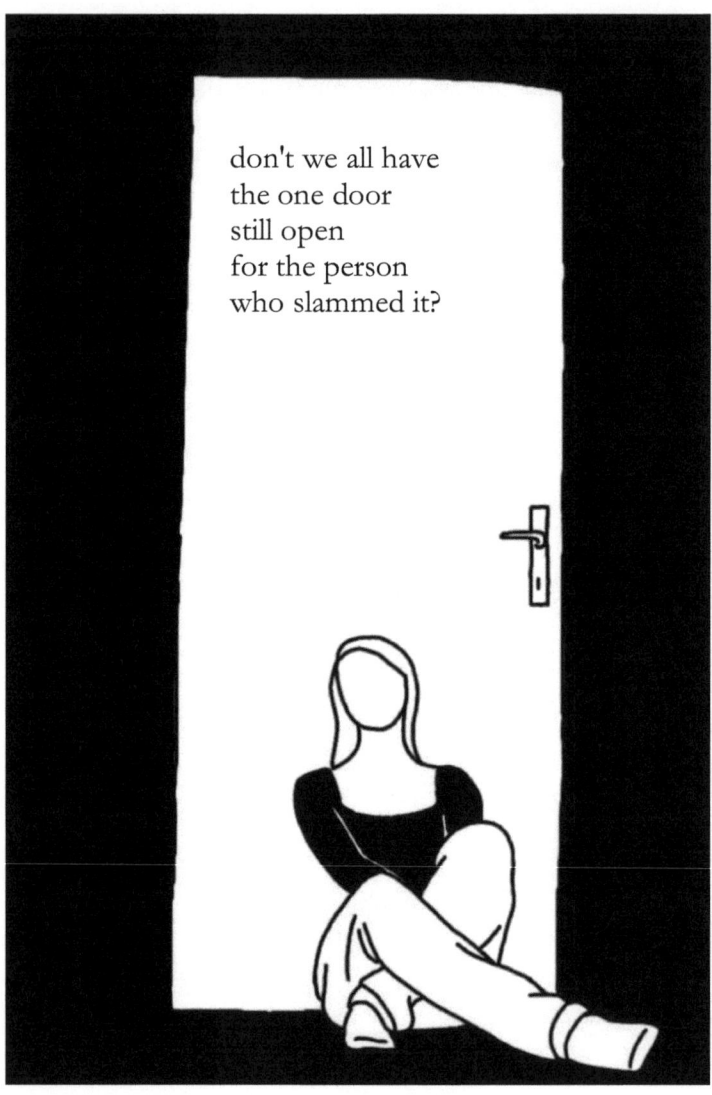

don't we all have
the one door
still open
for the person
who slammed it?

it is time to
throw away the key
in the resulting lake of tears

all those things…

when the lake dries out
and the key finally found
you will see
you won't need it anymore

all those things…

have you noticed
you cover impressment with envy?

you can do these things too
you know?

do not ignore warning signs
do not discover a dead end over and over again
do not humiliate yourself
do not make yourself false hope

accept it, end it and move on

never let the people around you
be the reasons for your living

they will leave, they always do

stop making your life harder
by asking questions
nobody will ever have answers for

you know what i mean

there will always be people
who hurt you

you should not be one of them

cut of people
who annoys you
at a point
it is just unhealthy

all those things…

don't keep people
you have a past with
but now no future

how to let go of someone (without blocking)
because everyone says so but does not explain how

☐ unadd from snapchat.

☐ block und unblock on instagram[1].

☐ delete on any social media (yes, even pinterest, youtube, reddit, etc.).

☐ delete chat on whatsapp (delete it, but you can transfer the chat as a memory in an usb stick).

☐ delete the number.

☐ put everything that reminds you of this person in the bin or in a box (this means also the lamp you still use and the hoodie you like to wear. and do not forget the scarf and the book the person's mother gave you).

☐ if you choose the box: **do not name it!** hide it somewhere you cannot easily see or get it. you have to be looking for it to find it again.

☐ remake the memories with other people or yourself.

☐ wait.

---

[1] life-hack for not only unfollow the person but also make her/him unfollow you because seeing her/him liking your post does not help at all

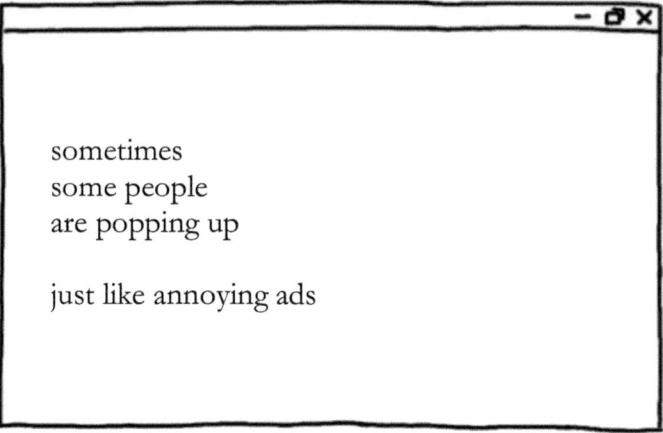

sometimes
some people
are popping up

just like annoying ads

there are two types of humans

1. the one who plays an important part in a chapter of your life for character development

2. the one who leads you to the above-named person

caution: what role the person has does not matter

it simply cannot be done over night
be patient with yourself

the dumbest way a person can get is
to believe people can change
even if they have proven the opposite

how to be positive
because everyone tells you so, even your psychologist, but does not explain how

- every time you experience something truly happy get yourself something that reminds you of it. if you are not doing well, relive the moment.
  update your "happy moment" with the most recent or strongest one.

- remove "bad blood" by discussing why it is even there with the person. sometimes it goes well. sometimes it does not. but remember, you gave your best and did everything you could. it is their loss, not yours.

- remind yourself you went through a similar phase and you will again.

- count those good things which are going to happen if you are through this phase.

stop blaming them for not being able to read
your mind

fake it until you make it does not work
with feelings

by trying to love again
do not self-sabotage
it will hurt both

how to enjoy moments
because everyone tells you so but does not explain how

- do not try to manipulate by thinking about the past or even the future

- enjoy the view, the city, the people

- count the good things in your life

- do not start creating solution for problems

some of us are able to enjoy the moment
some of us will be able to enjoy the moment
don't you worry, soon you can too

you are ashamed of how you acted
when you were younger?

congratulations, you matured

you do not want to be someone
you want to be *like* someone

be your own version

what does it mean to be yourself?

when all your different faces become one
and you are comfortable with it

all those things…

you evolve
you will never be like this again

you like every kinds of bodies

your own one should not be an exception

all those things…

write your thoughts down
and you will see
what demons you will have slayed

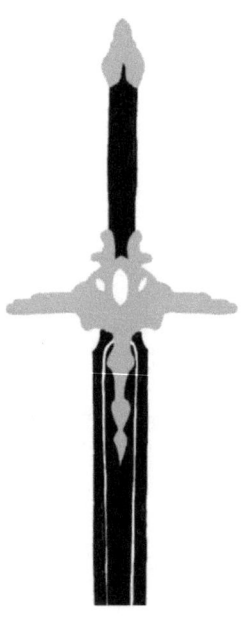

oh dear,
you have the look
you have the personality
you would be way to powerful with
self-confidence

all those things…

time does not heal your wounds
but time teaches you how to overcome them

stop hate
start accept
and soon
you will love

- yourself

all those things…

get out there
your soulmate is certainly not next door

you will overcome your personal doomsday
promised

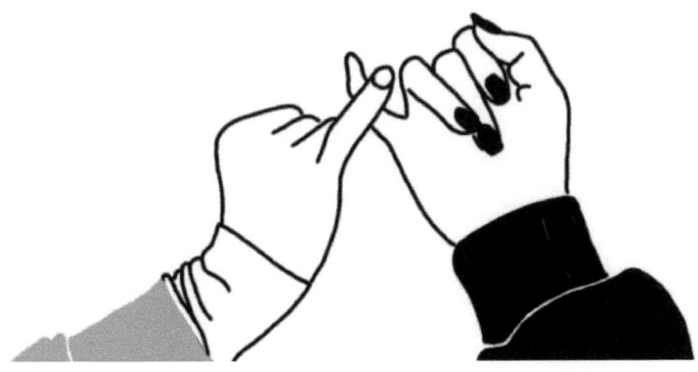

the personal doomsday
(german: "der persönliche weltuntergang")

this is how i call the lowest point of our lives
this is the period where we prefer the end of
the world over the current situation
this is the life changing moment
this is the individual scale of pain

just because she and he and the stranger
might have experienced war
does not mean you feeling pain from words
cannot be a 10 out of 10

this is a different generation
this is a different standard
this is a different life

this is human being

acknowledgements

enormous thanks to the people who intensively
supported this poetry book:

Xenia
for being my friend since kindergarten and for inspiring
me how to take more care of our planet.

Shpresa
for your feedback to each poem. i am so glad you
"changed your mindset".

Riccarda
for making me wake up on mondays, what would i do at
school without you?

Flavio
for helping me with the other perspective and for your
opinions to several questions i asked.

Sharon
for your excitement for this book. i cross my fingers for
you and your sport career.

Anna "Nanamey"
for your help at the final step with your own book
experience. i would have panicked without you.

Ms Armstrong, Ms Wolf and Mr Eser
for your support, patience, knowledge and corrections. i
probably would embarrass myself without you.

special thanks:

Felicia
for being there for me when i hit rock bottom. you are
my zodiac sister.

Mike
for being the first one who seriously helped me when i
needed someone and for telling me, i will live the best life
in 10 years. it ended up being just 5!

Cédric "Turbos Skeron"
for your cheering, jokes, patience, love and for making
me cry tears of joy. may your plans soon be achieved.

Céline and Berfin
for your lovely feedbacks, comments and hype.

every person who broke me
for pushing me off the edge. i am proud of who i am
today.

You
for giving this poetry book and me a chance. i danced
when i got your order.

instagram: @irono.yami
e-mail address: irono.yami@outlook.com
#allthosethingspoems

all those things…

irono.yami

third printing

Printing, bookbinding and launching process:
BoD – Books on Demand, Norderstedt

ISBN: 978-3-7534-0775-3